Fiction by J. Paul Pemsler

One Dozen ...with Everything (2006)
short stories

The More of Me

poems of life, love and ageing

J. Paul Pemsler

ISBN: 978-1-4834-8477-8 (sc)
ISBN: 978-1-4834-8476-1 (e)

Because of the dynamic nature of the Internet, any web addresses or links contained in this book may have changed since publication and may no longer be valid. The views expressed in this work are solely those of the author and do not necessarily reflect the views of the publisher, and the publisher hereby disclaims any responsibility for them.

Any people depicted in stock imagery provided by Getty Images are models, and such images are being used for illustrative purposes only. Certain stock imagery © Getty Images.

Lulu Publishing Services rev. date: 05/11/2018

Cover photograph, Solar Flare, by Suzanne Pemsler

Photo of author by b&b Photography, Boise, Idaho

For Xan, Toby, Carmen, Marisa, Clover, and Poppy

"Fear not each sudden sound and shock,
'Tis of the wave and not the rock ..."

Henry Wadsworth Longfellow

Contents

INAMORATAS

The More Of Me

There must be more of me
For I am not enough to smell the spring,
Or watch clouds rob luster from the glade
And fill the brook with dimpled ring.

More than me needs feel ocean waves
Invade a summer's lang'rous beach,
Then gently leave their treasure spoils
To roll far back, far out of reach.

It is beyond my means
To watch the fall calliope sing
And see sunlit shafts emerge
'Twixt falling mustard wing.

It can't be me alone who watches snowflakes
Fluff onto a window's ledge
And heap upon the lawn so high
It bows the massive hedge.

But when my love will come to me
Clad in pitch-black tresses,
Then she will make the more of me
And I each season bless.

Summer Romance

Hearts bred warm by summer's sun
Oft chill and shrink to winter's gray
Enchanted evenings and lengthy nights
Turn to but another day.

Hearts bred warm by moonlit nights
Lie 'neath snowy blankets lost
To await again excited hearts
When springtime brings to thaw the frost.

The Other Rose

I am the other rose
In my lady's book so neatly pressed
Side by side with another
Must I for countless ages rest
Whose fragrance at one special time
Smelled every bit as sweet as mine

I am the other heart
Whose passion she did know
Enraptured by her cunning
No longer free to go
For e'er must I repose
Within the capsule of that rose

Pressed flowers in their time
Wither and decay with age
As hearts grow old and ill
Unfed by love's sweet rage
Untaxed to live their life
Amid her nect'ral strife

Oh, withered rose that I shall become
Petals brown and dried, my fragrance spent
Replaced by cadaverous effluvium
All the charm the gods had lent
In long years interim
Will you know me from my twin?

Seek me not in my stature
For I shall shrivel as I die
Nor seek to recall upon
Which leaf of text I did lie
But 'neath the calyx torn apart
Find me in the blighted heart

Take it in your hand
With sweet remembrance smile
Then plant it in your heart
And in death's sweet while
Shall it bloom anew and your carrion fill
With love's unending fragrant 'still

Spring Poem

I tried to write a poem to you
But words got in the way
When I began to sing my thoughts
The tune went far astray
So I smiled at jonquils dancing
That's what I meant to say

I tried to give you all my love
But life got in the way
And I went about my calling
To keep the wolves at bay
Is it too late to wish, my love,
To hand you this bouquet?

Now, mirrors mock our countenance
The two of us this way
While age draws shadows o'er our lives
And minds begin to stray
But still within your eyes are smiles
No dancing jonquils can convey!

Very Male, Very 1960's

It was very male, it was very sixties:
He had worked late, arrived home
To find the kids tucked in, asleep,
Wife in bed, head-hit-the-pillow exhausted.
In the kitchen, he opened the fridge
Whose small light illuminated the darkened room,
Removed the wax paper-covered supper plate,
Sat silently eating a roast beef sandwich,
Downing a nightcap of Budweiser from the bottle.

Sated, he headed toward the stairs,
Halted, compelled by a wave of love
Surging in innocence from within,
Flowing upward step by step,
Covering his wife and children like a blanket,
Insulating them with infinite safekeeping.

He began to climb the stairs wearily,
Knowing the blanket was ephemeral.

Anniversary

Anniversaries come yet never go
Mounding like cubes of sugar
Pyramid form, sweetening life
Paving passages to the peak
With luscious icing betwixt
Softening that chancy tread
To reach the final stage
Of death and beyond
Where eternal certainty
Is but to await the other

POETASTERS

I Prefer Prose

Prose is substantial,
Mortar and bricks
Build structures of lives,
Landscaping dynasties
Of diverse design,
Twigging their entities.

Poetry builds through
Cobwebs and sunbeams,
Floating above meaning,
Shimmering, dancing
Before questioning eyes,
Only hinting at revelations.

I prefer prose.

Iambs-R-Not-Us

I do not wish to write in rhyme,
Each iamb is a heinous crime
Why stifle dearest thoughts divine
Conveyed by muses in their prime?

Alliterations make me weep
I'd toss them on an old scrapheap
It's time to free us from that sneap
We're not a herd of baaing sheep

We need a verse that's blank and free
'Twould let us write true poesy
And scramble words in two and three
To form a stratus repartee

There's this mount I'd like to climb
With lyrics by O. Hammerstein
High in those Alps I'd never pine
While verse resigns as Swiss bells chime

I'd make it in a quantum leap
Where air is thin and thoughts are deep
I've meters to destroy before I sleep
Sweep them away before I sleep

Why Did I Wait So Long?

Why did I wait so long
to accept this assignment?
I should have begun at the end of my poetic journey, bored
    through my poems backwards,
through deconstruction and reconstruction,
beyond blank verse, free verse and adverse.

When I look at the centripetal force
of my poetic life,
I see but a journey, sometimes only an itinerary.
Prisoner of lyrical confinement,
I've burrowed under the floors of my cell,
stumbled over forms in tunnels, stopped, recited,
resumed my journey.

The thing about it is that all poetic souls are interchangeable:
Seeking what is new, we dig deeper only into ourselves.

HAPPENINGS

Incantation

I'm weary of fighting the forces of evil
Surveying barbicans awash with mass carnage
I'm exhausted from raising my indignation
At newspaper headlines and TV newscasters
Why can't I be yogic, serenely dispel it,
Observe it from far off, nod every so often

So that's what will happen to my crumbling planet
I want to say sorry pal, no more petitions
Not even just causes, my ethic's on furlough
Yet, you know me dear friend, I'll cobble it together
With all of my stamina writhing in loathing
Hand me now quickly that damned new petition

I'll sign without reading in protest of roses
Whose bouquet of fragrance alarms my position
And floats me up skyward where thoughts can make
    circles
Where love tugs me onward to saner conditions
'Till attars are faded and petals turn moldy
And viewing is lost to the sense of the horror

First Tuesday in November

Election day arrives in the newly dark of standard time
When lollygagging afternoons are cleaved by clocks
an hour too short
When after work, on crowded head-lit streets,
I drive to a polling booth in a middle school gym
Cued by tiny print the names dare choice
and my finger dances like God's reach to Adam

So my ripple grows to a wave and sums flow
through cables to TVs where pollsters examine
Spoors of voters foretelling victory and defeat
Through the night I wake for late results, my life on hold
Seeking whether this nation can long endure
Feeling it will somehow survive

Alt-Thanksgiving

Thanksgiving? To whom? For what?
It's all on your Internet – check it out
Thanksgiving to John Rolfe and wife Pocohontas
who created the mild tobacco blend that sold like tea in
England
Thanksgiving to the slaves in Virginia who grew the
tobacco
that made the cash that funded the New England harvest
feast
Thanksgiving to the surgeon general, hundreds of years
from being born,
and scores more 'till condemning that mild, mild tobacco

Thanksgiving to Sarah Hale who made the myth
that prompted Lincoln to make the feast a national holiday
Thanksgiving to Squanto (never heard of him when I went
to school)
The maître d' who planted the corn, who trapped the
game,
who ran the feast, whose people died from diseases
brought by the colonists
Long gone, too, is G. Washington's cherry tree chop – all
taken away
What have we left with which to fight the terrorists?
Damn shame, damn shame

Requiem For Many

Have you noticed, my dear, that *Many* has disappeared
    from both Oxford and Webster?
Oh, I think it's a conspiracy
What will become of the *Multiple* songs and poems with
    the word *Many*?
Remember that Oklahoma! hit *Many a New Day*?
It's in there a dozen times
Those were the good old days, don't you think?

The last time *Many* was spoken on NPR was in 2015 when
    a guest – never invited again – slipped it in
Multiple journalists and newscasters attended *Many's*
    burial and solemnly swore never to use that word again

Numerous was at the burial and hid behind a tombstone
    lest it would also be declared dead
Perhaps the mathematicians will reclaim *Many* as the
    "*Manyplication*" table to get even with those straying
    grammarians
One hopes

I guess I'll just go on mourning for that simple word *Many*
    with *Multiple* uses

PERCEPTIONS

Merry Christmas, Mr. Brown

I do not like you, Mr. Brown
In fact, I hate you Mr. B
I do not like the way you frown
Or how you always glare at me

I'd like to punch you on the snout
And shake your vest, you silly fool
Yet I must be content to pout
Aware the time of year is Yule

Rumpled View

Rumpelstiltskin died for our sins and more
When he stomped his foot through that palace floor
For all we misfits who'll grab at a chance
Take a shot at wealth or perhaps romance
While we wait for fame to open the door

Our savior was lucky to fast expire
To the underworld in a burst of ire
In one grandiloquent thrust of disgust
But we must live out our lives – we must
And dream thoughts of what will never transpire

Daily, the Wall Street Journal is fraught
With huge gains of stocks we never bought
We linger in Harvard Square all harried
Ogling students with whom we've not tarried
What hath that knave Rupeltstiltskin wrought?

Come pray with me for Rumpel's soul
Entombed in hell with gnomes and ghouls
For in his salvation we find our own
And hurry back to hearth and home
Renouncing all our errant goals

Woman Walking With Vase

A vase secure under her left arm,
Her right hand a fist 'round one handle
No idle vase this to be propped
In some corner of a darkened hall

Of a single color, pumpkin perhaps
Did she design it, throw it on a wheel?
No Grecian urn of Keats she bares
Might it hold the ashes of a cherished life?

The Man Is Ill

The man is ill: attention must be paid
His heart grows faint, legs shake from a chill
A homeless man: care must not be delayed

We found him that way, his coat all unmade
At the top of Carbury Hill
The man is ill: attention must be paid

We carried him here where triage is made
Please help straight away, his hands tremble still
A homeless man: care must not be delayed

Dear nurse: his breath grows faint, he is afraid
Come move in the gurney, please if you will
The man is ill: attention must be paid

Dear doctor: do not your duties evade
His breathing has stopped, he lies there quite still
A homeless man: care must not be delayed

Dear man: I can see him, I need no tirade
I've patients to treat, he seems quite tranquil
The man's not ill: attention must be *payed*
A homeless man: care can be delayed

Ta, Ta, Now

It's all about dignity, she said
I mean I don't give a damn
If what I write is true
It's how people read it, how they treat me
That's the bottom line, isn't it?

When you get to a certain age, you know
You see them look right past you
You wear your best clothes and suffer high heels
Still you're not there – it's a wonder they don't
Knock you down you're so invisible

I preen sometimes and in more ways than one:
"Hello world, I'm still here" I know deep down that I matter
But at least humanity could hint at it once in a while
Just a reminder or two, some sort of recognition
Enough to take home and nurse for a few days

I was someone once: I was relevant
No, I didn't win a Pulitzer
Though my third book got good notices
I could have been nominated, but you know me
I was never political

Would you believe someone had the nerve to tell me to
    submit a poem to *Spare Change*?
Can you imagine?
I mean people read that paper
For God's sake, they'd think I'm homeless
How many more years can I go on before I become a
    cipher in some nursing home?

Well, it was good seeing you
Ta, ta, now – I've got to see my agent
At least, I think he's still my agent

JOURNEY

Magic Portals, 1952

Mondays at six I breathed a different air
Rich with a contagion I could not perceive
When Larry, Rhoda and I walked past
The Washington Square Park bench
Where my first poem wrote itself
Headed to the Cedar Tavern for dinner
Then returning to NYU for evening
Lectures on Advanced Organic Chemistry

At Cedar, we slunk into high-backed oaken booths
And Rhoda, a WASP, hurled invectives at
Catholicism, only to write an apologia seven years later
Of how she came to marry a Catholic
And where I learned a Martini had an olive
And a Manhattan a cherry.

In graduate school, smelling the odor of Chemistry
Laboratories, feeling the heat of Bunsen burners
My nose neither sensed the odor of linseed from
Willem de Kooning, Mark Rothko, Jackson Pollock
Nor felt the heat of passion from
Kenneth Koch, John Ashbery, Frank O'Hara
There in Cedar Tavern they also sat,
I would learn later, there at the brink of
Abstract Expressionism and founding
The New York School of Poets

There, at the brink of my own existence
Riding the subway from Spring Street
To the 174th street IRT station in the Bronx
I exalted in the seductive mushroom cloud
Of the Atom Bomb, reading texts
On particle physics and Candide

Standing at the front of the first car
Peering out the window at the red, amber and
Green signal lights in the tunnel conduit that
Shaped my eight-year college journey, finally
Spewing me onto a Plane to Oak Ridge, Tennessee
Where I had scant time to shop the Fourth Avenue
Book Store whose block-long sign proclaimed
"Books Are The Keys to Magic Portals"

LATER YEARS

Gather Ye Crow's Feet

Age is but beauty clothed in textured wrap
Where every crease unfurls a soul's sweet map

Arrays of smooth faces but deceive
Display no hint of what mind can conceive

So harken maidens fair with face sublime:
Gather no rosebuds, just pray you'll decline

Corrugated Annie

So me face is full o' wrinkles and folds
'Tis but the good Lord's sign o' bein' old
Them's got their faces like a baby's arse
I say they've got n'er drib o' class
Je's wait a tad 'till they've chin whiskers too
'N won't be usin' rouge nor lipstick, nooo

Equinox

It is the equinox when we awake
To pendulum's surprise of seasons change
Where stereopticon disjointed scenes
Slowly converge as deepest hues arrange
Landscapes, where daybreak chills to capitulate
To midday febrile surges within souls
Of the elderly to conquer dawn's languor

Without, fauna scurry about, insights
Aroused by primal anxious thoughts
Of vast expanses of frozen tundra

Ageing me? I contemplate the
Whereabouts of winter boots

POSTLUDE

Perhaps

I don't spend much time thinking
About life cycles and meaning
Or road maps for living
Or what my legacy will be
I live in the innocence of radio days
When we laughed at Gracie Allen's
Jokes long before the punch lines arrived
When things were so far down
But FDR smiled so you knew
That they had to go up
Even through a bitter war

I tend to put off serious thoughts
Preferably until it's too late
Until mourners define my life's voyage
Far better than I'd be able
Oh, I know some day as they say
When it's least expected
Questions will become manifest
And their brazen gaze will challenge me

Perhaps I'll ponder those reflective things
That people said when their guards fell
When unadorned truth confronted them
As it will then confront me
Perhaps

Elder Residence

Elder is the dance we do
As Mori calls the tune
Rev'lers sport what steps we knew
To drive away the gloom

Botox is the smile we wear
To hide the creeping years
Cronies watch our efforts bear
Scant hope to banish tears

All of us the courtly set
Conspire and bow upon the stage
None of us has learned quite yet
What's writ upon life's final page

Dignitas our lofty peak
Irrelevance we abjure
From deep within our souls we speak
Of heaven's lone primogeniture

Yet we must continue on
This *Elder* dance we do
For what is left if we sojourn
But shadows of old derring-do?

Sashay with me by waning moon
Come do that do-si-do again
With *Elder* on the way to doom
Here in God's Great Holding Pen

Last Vacation

This is my last vacation and I've chosen it well
There's a large screen TV, it's like an IMAX there
I think I know all the actors, but I forget their
    appellations
Once I knew the names of movies, the characters
    as well
I may have been in one once, perhaps heretofore
Maybe yesterday or last week

It's easeful in my hotel
I rock a great deal, even when I'm not in a chair
I must be in anguish, the actors keep giving me
    medication – all colors – and then I just stare
Soon another flick will start – I hope I haven't seen
    it before

De Novo

When everything is over it is really not
When the unexpected bursts forth
crying more, there will be more
When the wellspring of inspiration pours
forth a glistening brook of syllables
my poem will erupt a further stanza

When my journey ends
there will yet be a coda
to lead me to my grave
where silence finally secludes